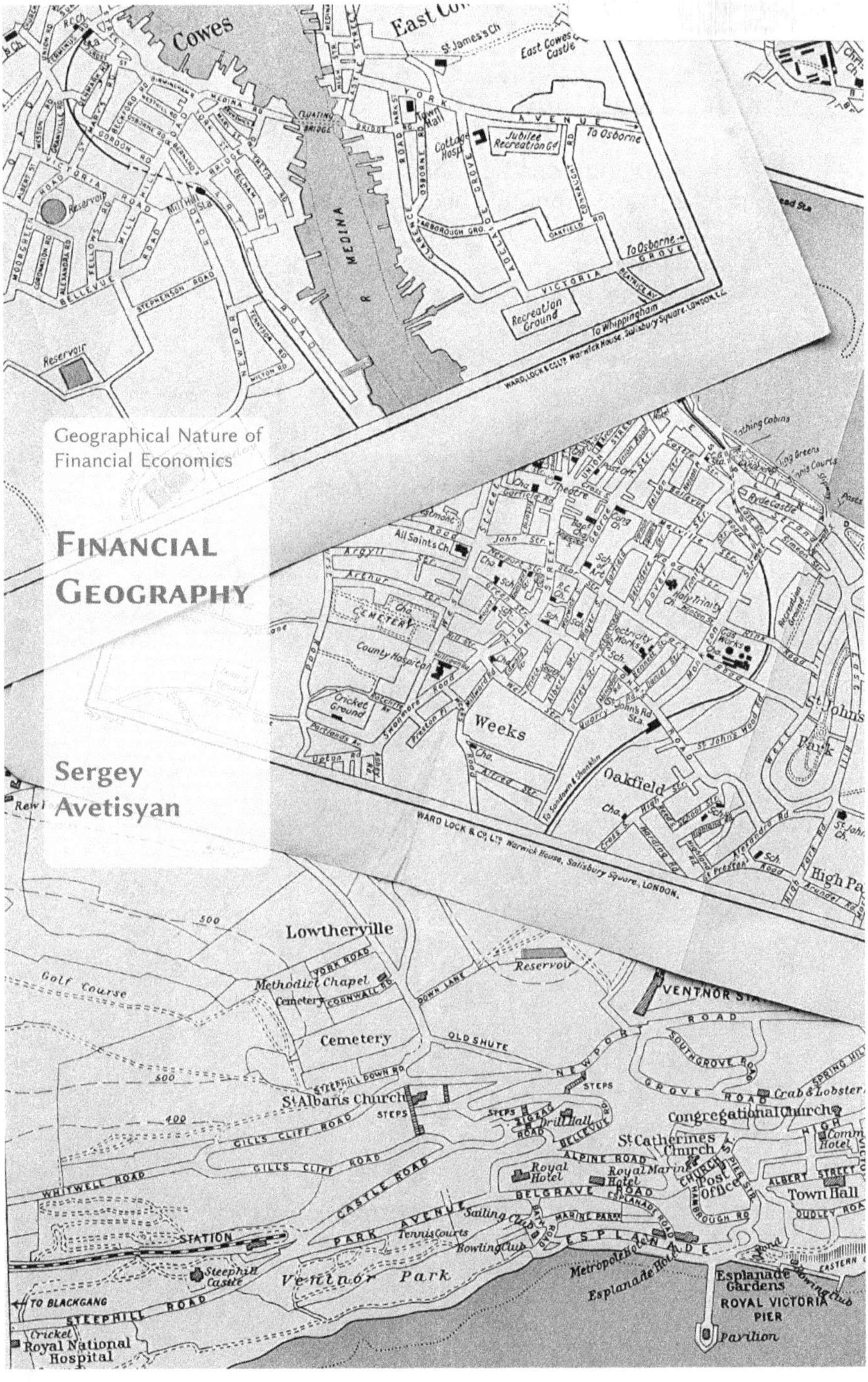

Geographical Nature of
Financial Economics

FINANCIAL
GEOGRAPHY

Sergey
Avetisyan

© 2019 *Sergey Avetisyan*
ALL RIGHTS RESERVED.

For more information about permission to reproduce selections from this book, write to `avetisyan.sergej@gmail.com`.
Second Version[1]
E-book created November 6, 2019
Cover design: *by me*
Image sources: `canva.com`

ISBN: 9781696867474
Write to `avetisyan.sergej@gmail.com` or visit website `www.avetisyansergey.com`.

---

[1] *This Essay should not be regarded as representing the views of Central Bank of Armenia. The views in this essay are those of the author and should not be interpreted as those of Central Bank of Armenia.*

Financial Geography ESSAY

Sergey Avetisyan

November 6, 2019

Contents

Contents		**4**
1	Preface	5
2	Introduction	6
3	Literature review	8
4	Financial geography	11
5	Financial stability	13
6	Arguments	16
7	Conclusion	17
Bibliography		**18**
Concept index		**24**

Chapter 1

Preface

The evolving architecture of the financial world pays attention to space structure of financial activities. I elaborate on the literature about the role of space in financial economics. This essay is focuses on a question: *"How to grasp the conundrum of financial geography?"* The purpose of this essay is to bring together some of the more salient similarities between economic geography and financial economics. Financial economic models have not been primarily concerned with the question of spatial distribution of economic activity, since they often implicitly assume that markets ensure a geographically well-distributed economy. The essay has three related objectives. The first is to provide a primer on the field of *financial geography*. The second, and perhaps the most significant, objective is to convince a wider audience of the novelty and relevance of this field. The third objective is to argue that this approach is potentially suitable to understanding the field.

Chapter 2

Introduction

The first understanding in writing the essay was to find a center of gravity: two concepts (economic geography and financial economics); help to understand and give coherence to conceptual discussion of financial geography.

Financial geography is concerned with the roles of finance, money and markets in the restructuring of economic world. Financial geography research focuses on how such restructuring has uneven impacts across space, and also the ways in which space and place are mobilized in the production of financial markets and processes. Some examples of the specialities of finance include financial exclusion, regional inequalities due to financial activities, differential connectivity of global, local financial flows, networks, the rise of new onshore, and offshore financial centres.

More than acting as a neutral lubricant in the economic system, financial markets, actors and instruments shape the development and life chances of people and communities across regions and localities. While some have argued that globalization and new information and communication technologies have rendered geography irrelevant, financial geographers contest that space and place remain crucial to the financial system in shaping financial decisions, allocation of capital, regulatory frameworks of global financial markets, and their unequal outcomes.

What are the most promising research topics for future financial geography? And equally, what are

the most important challenges facing financial geography?

"[...] I'm not going to suggest the most promising topics for future research in financial geography or the geography of finance. Even when I was a younger academic, I would have ignored such advice. Perhaps I ignored advice when I should have listened. [...] The point I want to make is that you can claim a certain status or space by virtue of your discipline. But it is really about adding value rather than being a certain type of academic from a certain type of discipline. So my advice on this point goes as follows: it's not about proving that a geographical perspective is important to your academic colleagues, it's about weaving geography into explanations of how financial markets, agents, and organisations function such that your insights have value [1]*."*

— Clark, Gordon L

So, my motivation is to summarize open questions in financial geography; *"What we lose when the geographical aspects of economic activities aren't involved in financial stability analyses?," "Does monetary policy have an impact on regional disparities?," "Does commercial banks branches distribution, have an impact on non-performing loans?," "Why should the geographical distribution of banks' decision centers matter?," "How commercial bank make a decision for branch location?."*

The remainder of this article is organized as follows: The next section discuss the literature based on financial stability and financial geography. The essay moves on to look at thought of several authors about distance impact on inter-bank relationships. The next section addresses on theoretical arguments. The final section offers an summery of literature and some conclusions.

---

[1] *Quoted from "Interview by Dariusz Wójcik and Theodor Cojoianu, School of Geography and the Environment, Oxford University." (available on: http://www.fingeo.net/clark-gordon-l-professor-and-director-smith-school-of-enterprise-and-the-environment-oxford-university/)*

Chapter 3

Literature review

Economic models have not been primarily concerned with the question of spatial distribution of economic activity, since they often implicitly assume that markets ensure a geographically well-distributed economy.
New economic geography support a myriad of methods for time-space-structural analysis ([Mitze, 2012], [Nickel et al., 2005], [Wilson, 2012]). The bulk of geographical writing about finance and money consists of sectoral contributions. These take a comparatively narrow segment and penetrate it at varying depth. Most writing is of article length which sets its restrictions. The field at large has become popular only since the late 1980s [Laulajainen, 2005].

This literature review examines essential characteristics of space and financial stability (Table 5.1). Some research has identified a difference between "bank-based" and "market-based" financial systems ([Zysman, 1984], [Leyshon and Thrift, 1998]) argue that geography is the important in the evolution of money and there has been a failure to be suitably sensitive to the interplay between money, space and place, to see that monetary forms, practices and institutions are contingent in both space and time, and that money has often evolved in order to solve more general problems of time-space co-ordination. Generally, money allows social relationships and must be extended across space and time. Usually financial stability researchers don't concentrat on space aspects of economic activities; they don't use time-space-structural analysis.

[Brevoort and Wolken, 2009] examining literature on how the relative locations of banks and their customers have changed over time. We can consider that the banks, through their loan decisions, are a crucial command centre in the economy that affects most other aspect of the economy.

[Petersen and Rajan, 2002] in *"Does Distance Still Matter? The Information Revolution in Small Business Lending"* demonstrate the distance between small firms and their lenders is increasing, and they are communicating in more impersonal ways. After documenting these systematic changes, they argue that they do not arise from small firms locating differently, consolidation in the banking industry, or biases in the sample. The paper makes a number of contributions. For one, it focuses on new metrics for informational closeness: physical distance and method of communication. Others have used distance as a proxy for informational asymmetry ([Coval and Moskowitz, 1999], [Garmaise and Moskowitz, 1999],
[Grinblatt and Keloharju, 2001]).

[Knyazeva and Knyazeva, 2012] in *"Does being your bank's neighbor matter?"* provides new evidence on the role of distance between banks and borrowers in bank lending. Knyazeva argues that delegated monitors face higher costs of collecting information about non local borrowers due to the difficulty of obtaining and verifying soft information over distances. Further, the higher information collection and monitoring costs associated with distance should be reflected in loan terms. Empirically, loan spreads are increasing in the distance between borrowers and lenders. Finally, banks are more likely to include covenant provisions or require collateral when lending to borrowers located far away. **Theoretical view give us two theories about distance and interest rate relationship.** Two theories predict opposing impacts of distance on pricing and size of credit: the information hypothesis predicts interest rates to rise as distance increases since asymmetric information issues worsens. On the other hand, the local market power view predicts interest rates to fall in distance because banks enjoy less of a monopoly position.

Two theories predict opposing impacts of distance on pricing and size of credit, the existing banking literature finds contradicting results to this question, likely due to the endogenous nature of location choice.

[Petersen and Rajan, 2002], [Degryse and Ongena, 2005], [Agarwal and Hauswald, 2010],

[Knyazeva and Knyazeva, 2012],[Bellucci et al., 2013], [Colonnello and Herpfer, 2016] exploit exogenous shocks to the distance between corporate borrowers and banks to analyze the role of distance in commercial bank lending. [Colonnello and Herpfer, 2016] conclude that a reduction in driving time between banks and their borrowers is associated with an increase in interest rates. Analysis of the role of distance in banking by exploring the reason why one might expect distance, or more specifically geographic proximity, to play in important role in the provision, delivery, and use of banking services.

Chapter 4

Financial geography

According to [Martin and Pollard, 2017], physical distance may be the most obvious measure of "proximity" between banks and customer firms, it is not necessarily the most meaningful or relevant, particularly when either the bank or its customer firms have multiple geographical locations.

Especially in the provision of credit, when a bank has multiple branches, the concept of "distance" becomes complex. The bank's branches may play different roles in providing services to borrowers, with one branch serving as a point of personal contact with a firm seeking a loan, another housing the decision makers who approve or deny the loan, and yet another which has responsibility for loan monitoring operations ([Brevoort and Wolken, 2009]).

Similarly, for firms with multiple locations, it is not necessarily clear which location in the most relevant for obtaining financial services. Each location may play a role, and the importance of each may differ according to the nature of the financial service being sought.

The earlier works of (for example, [Zazzaro, 1997], [Alessandrini et al., 2005]) make a distinction between *"operational distance,"* the physical distance between a bank and its customers, and *"functional distance,"* defined as the distance between a bank's decision-making centre and the bank's branch. Functional distance thus captures the spatial remoteness between the different hierarchical layers of a banking organization.

Using network analysis techniques, and focusing on the Italian banking system, they show that the overall interconnectedness of geographical credit markets has significantly increased over time, whether measured at the regional or provincial level. They go on to demonstrate that within this process, there has been a growing and marked centralization of the system within a few northern Italian banking centres to the detriment of the southern credit markets and regions.

Their study highlights the importance of the concept of distance, especially that of functional distance, in shaping the relationships between banks and local borrowers, and how this has worked in recent years to intensify the country's core–periphery financial and banking divide, with adverse consequences for the small business sector in the south of the country.

Chapter 5
Financial stability

[Allen and Wood, 2006] define a financially stable system as simply one: "which is not prone to episodes of financial instability."

What we lose when don't include the geographical aspects of economic activities in banking stability analyses? Simple answer is *"deregulation and technological change have reduced the transaction costs that led to the dominance of local financial service suppliers, leading some to question whether distance still matters in banking. This debate has been particularly intense in small business banking, where transactions costs are believed to be particularly high"* ([Brevoort and Wolken, 2009]).

It is rare to find an economics text in which space is studied as an important subject. As argued by [Krugman, 1997], this is probably because economists lacked a model embracing both increasing returns and imperfect competition, the two basic ingredients of the formation of the economic landscape, as shown by the pioneering work of [Hotelling, 1929], [Lösch, 1940], [Isard, 1956].

According to [Gallup et al., 1999], location and climate have large effects on income levels and income growth, through their effects on transport costs, disease burdens, and agricultural productivity, among other channels. Furthermore, geography seems to be a factor in the choice of economic policy itself.

From a historic perspective, one can broadly distinguish

between three types of financial instability. First, there is volatility-based instability. A second type of instability is stress-based instability. Lastly, there are instances of crises-based financial instability.

If in fiscal policy geographical factors are more or less clear, in monetary economics it is open question. [Ron Martin, 1999] has been one of the forerunners in providing invaluable theoretical and empirical insights into advancing our knowledge of the geographies of money. Continuing in this vein, [Ron Martin, 1999]'s book *"Money and the Space Economy"* brings together a selection of essays from geographers and economists whose remit is concerned with the geography of money.

At last, according to [Cohen, 1998] **"What do we mean by monetary geography?"**

"Although the term is not conventional, it actually encompasses much of what discussions of global monetary relations are all about. Most fundamentally, "monetary geography" refers to the spatial organization of currency relations-how monetary domains are configured and governed. Whether we recognize it or not, we all carry around cognitive images of how currency spaces are organized; and these images, or mental maps, in turn shape the way we routinely think about the role of money in world affairs."

Table 5.1: Literature structur

Financial geography	Distance relationship in banking	Commercial banks location analyses
[Leyshon and Thrift, 1998]	[Bellucci et al., 2013]	[Brealey and Kaplanis, 1996]
[Cohen, 1998]	[Beck et al., 2015]	[Boufounou, 1995]
[Ron Martin, 1999]	[Alessandrini et al., 2009a]	[Soenen, 1974]
[Laulajainen, 2005]	[Knyazeva and Knyazeva, 2012]	[Abbasi, 2003]
[Alessandrini et al., 2009a]	[Brevoort and Wolken, 2009]	[Fraser, 1978]
[Engelen and Faulconbridge, 2009]	[Cerqueiro et al., 2009]	[McAvoy, 2006]
[Lee et al., 2009]	[Alessandrini et al., 2009b]	[Goldberg and Grosse, 1994]
[Corrado and Corrado, 2015]	[De Blasio et al., 2009]	[Alamá and Tortosa-Ausina, 2012]
[Bieri, 2017]	[Ono et al., 2016]	[Okeahalam, 2009]
[Martin and Pollard, 2017]	[Brei and von Peter, 2017]	[Miliotis et al., 2002]
[Sokol, 2013]	[Degl'Innocenti et al., 2017]	[Hartman et al., 2001]
[Aalbers, 2015]	[Flögel, 2017]	[Nguyen, 2014]

Source: Author's own elaboration.

Chapter 6
Arguments

Does distance matter for financial stability? My arguments is structured as follows.

Distance can be a complex, multidimensional relational concept.

Literature suggest that the distance has an exogenous (endogenous) shock nature in banking structure.

Some authors estimate gravity equation for trade and banking side by side to show that the distance puzzle has a counterpart in international finance.

The intangibility easily gives the impression that the friction of distance the core of geography, will be marginal at best. And when the friction of distance is lost, the discipline also loses most of its foundations. This opinion implicitly assumes that the financial landscape is homogeneous. **However, the real financial landscape is not homogeneous at all, it is extremely heterogeneous and full of anomalies.**

In terms of policy implications, several authors confirm that the level of financial development increases with GDP. This raises the question regarding the qualitative nature of the interaction between regional financial stability and local institutions in the *"production process of financial development."*

Chapter 7
Conclusion

In the last four decades, the economics research frontier has been significantly transformed by a collection of new approaches that injected traditional economic geographical methodology. The changes in the financial geography research frontier assume future changes in economics. The new methods and concepts being adopted in economics coming from other sciences strongly suggest that economics will be substantially different in the future. The approaches presented in this literature review prove the role of regional disparities (regional aspects) to be fundamental in banking and credit research.

In this introductory essay, I first focus on the more general concept of financial geography. I classify the literature on into three parts: the first part of the literature focuses on demonstrating the role of space in financial economics and macroeconomic performance. The second part of the literature analyzes the relationship between banks and borrowers through triangles of distance and micro-financial conditions. The third part of the literature focuses on bank and facility location analysis.

Finally, highlighting important roles for both locality (market) and location (linkages within the network), and determining the outcomes of behavioural rules that shape equilibrium (spatial) landscapes and evolutionary paths, the above literature (Table 5.1) is closely related to new economic geography.

Bibliography

[Aalbers, 2015] Aalbers, M. B. (2015). Financial geography: introduction to the virtual issue. *Transactions of the Institute of British Geographers*, 40(2):300–305.

[Abbasi, 2003] Abbasi, G. Y. (2003). A decision support system for bank location selection. *International Journal of Computer Applications in Technology*, 16(4):202–210.

[Agarwal and Hauswald, 2010] Agarwal, S. and Hauswald, R. (2010). Distance and private information in lending. *Review of Financial studies*, page hhq001.

[Alamá and Tortosa-Ausina, 2012] Alamá, L. and Tortosa-Ausina, E. (2012). Bank branch geographic location patterns in spain: Some implications for financial exclusion. *Growth and Change*, 43(3):505–543.

[Alessandrini et al., 2005] Alessandrini, P., Croci, M., and Zazzaro, A. (2005). La geografia del potere bancario: il ruolo delle distanze funzionali (the geography of banking power: Role of function distance).

[Alessandrini et al., 2009a] Alessandrini, P., Fratianni, M., and Zazzaro, A. (2009a). *The changing geography of banking and finance*. Springer.

[Alessandrini et al., 2009b] Alessandrini, P., Presbitero, A. F., and Zazzaro, A. (2009b). Banks, distances and firms' financing constraints. *Review of Finance*, 13(2):261–307.

[Allen and Wood, 2006] Allen, W. A. and Wood, G. (2006). Defining and achieving financial stability. *Journal of Financial Stability*, 2(2):152–172.

[Beck et al., 2015] Beck, T., Ongena, S., and Sendeniz-Yuncu, I. (2015). Keep walking? geographical proximity, religion, and relationship banking. *Geographical Proximity, Religion, and Relationship Banking (July 24, 2015)*.

[Bellucci et al., 2013] Bellucci, A., Borisov, A., and Zazzaro, A. (2013). Do banks price discriminate spatially? evidence from small business lending in local credit markets. *Journal of Banking & Finance*, 37(11):4183–4197.

[Bieri, 2017] Bieri, D. (2017). Back to the future: Lösch, isard, and the role of money and credit in the space-economy. In *Regional Research Frontiers-Vol. 1*, pages 217–241. Springer.

[Boufounou, 1995] Boufounou, P. V. (1995). Evaluating bank branch location and performance: A case study. *European Journal of Operational Research*, 87(2):389–402.

[Brealey and Kaplanis, 1996] Brealey, R. A. and Kaplanis, E. C. (1996). The determination of foreign banking location. *Journal of International Money and Finance*, 15(4):577–597.

[Brei and von Peter, 2017] Brei, M. and von Peter, G. (2017). The distance effect in banking and trade. *BIS Working Papers No 658*.

[Brevoort and Wolken, 2009] Brevoort, K. P. and Wolken, J. D. (2009). Does distance matter in banking? In *The Changing Geography of Banking and Finance*, pages 27–56. Springer.

[Cerqueiro et al., 2009] Cerqueiro, G., Degryse, H., and Ongena, S. (2009). Distance, bank organizational structure, and lending decisions. In *The Changing Geography of Banking and Finance*, pages 57–74. Springer.

[Cohen, 1998] Cohen, B. J. (1998). *The geography of money.* Cornell University Press.

[Colonnello and Herpfer, 2016] Colonnello, S. and Herpfer, C. (2016). Do courts matter for firm value? evidence from the us court system. second draft. Technical report, IWH Discussion Papers.

[Corrado and Corrado, 2015] Corrado, G. and Corrado, L. (2015). The geography of financial inclusion across europe during the global crisis. *Journal of Economic Geography*, 15(5):1055–1083.

[Coval and Moskowitz, 1999] Coval, J. D. and Moskowitz, T. J. (1999). Home bias at home: Local equity preference in domestic portfolios. *The Journal of Finance*, 54(6):2045–2073.

[De Blasio et al., 2009] De Blasio, G., Omiccioli, M., Signorini, L. F., et al. (2009). Measuring the district effect. *Chapters.*

[Degl'Innocenti et al., 2017] Degl'Innocenti, M., Matousek, R., Sevic, Z., and Tzeremes, N. G. (2017). Bank efficiency and financial centres: Does geographical location matter? *Journal of International Financial Markets, Institutions and Money*, 46:188–198.

[Degryse and Ongena, 2005] Degryse, H. and Ongena, S. (2005). Distance, lending relationships, and competition. *The Journal of Finance*, 60(1):231–266.

[Engelen and Faulconbridge, 2009] Engelen, E. and Faulconbridge, J. (2009). Introduction: financial geographies—the credit crisis as an opportunity to catch economic geography's next boat? *Journal of economic geography*, 9(5):587–595.

[Flögel, 2017] Flögel, F. (2017). Distance and modern banks' lending to smes: ethnographic insights from a comparison of regional and large banks in germany. *Journal of Economic Geography*, 18(1):35–57.

[Fraser, 1978] Fraser, D. R. (1978). Bank location and the market evaluation of bank equity. *Atlantic Economic Journal*, 6(4):52–58.

[Gallup et al., 1999] Gallup, J. L., Sachs, J. D., and Mellinger, A. D. (1999). Geography and economic development. *International regional science review*, 22(2):179–232.

[Garmaise and Moskowitz, 1999] Garmaise, M. J. and Moskowitz, T. J. (1999). Adverse selection and re-trade. *The Center for Research in Security Prices, University of Chicago, working paper*, (507).

[Goldberg and Grosse, 1994] Goldberg, L. G. and Grosse, R. (1994). Location choice of foreign banks in the united states. *Journal of Economics and Business*, 46(5):367–379.

[Grinblatt and Keloharju, 2001] Grinblatt, M. and Keloharju, M. (2001). How distance, language, and culture influence stockholdings and trades. *The Journal of Finance*, 56(3):1053–1073.

[Hartman et al., 2001] Hartman, T. E., Storbeck, J. E., and Byrnes, P. (2001). Allocative efficiency in branch banking. *European Journal of Operational Research*, 134(2):232–242.

[Hotelling, 1929] Hotelling, H. (1929). Stability in competition. In *The Collected Economics Articles of Harold Hotelling*, pages 50–63. Springer.

[Isard, 1956] Isard, W. (1956). Location and space-economy.

[Knyazeva and Knyazeva, 2012] Knyazeva, A. and Knyazeva, D. (2012). Does being your bank's neighbor matter? *Journal of Banking & Finance*, 36(4):1194–1209.

[Krugman, 1997] Krugman, P. R. (1997). *Development, geography, and economic theory*, volume 6. MIT press.

[Laulajainen, 2005] Laulajainen, R. (2005). *Financial geography: a banker's view*. Routledge.

[Lee et al., 2009] Lee, R., Clark, G. L., Pollard, J., and Leyshon, A. (2009). The remit of financial geography—before and after the crisis. *Journal of Economic Geography*, 9(5):723–747.

[Leyshon and Thrift, 1998] Leyshon, A. and Thrift, N. (1998). Money/space: geographies of monetary transformation. *Capital & Class*, 22(2):182–185.

[Lösch, 1940] Lösch, A. (1940). The economics of location, 1954. *New Haven, Yale*.

[Martin and Pollard, 2017] Martin, R. and Pollard, J. (2017). *Handbook on the Geographies of Money and Finance*. Edward Elgar Publishing.

[McAvoy, 2006] McAvoy, M. R. (2006). How were the federal reserve bank locations selected? *Explorations in Economic History*, 43(3):505–526.

[Miliotis et al., 2002] Miliotis, P., Dimopoulou, M., and Giannikos, I. (2002). A hierarchical location model for locating bank branches in a competitive environment. *International transactions in operational research*, 9(5):549–565.

[Mitze, 2012] Mitze, T. (2012). *Empirical Modelling in Regional Science: Towards a Global Time–Space–Structural Analysis*, volume 657. Springer Science & Business Media.

[Nguyen, 2014] Nguyen, H.-L. Q. (2014). Do bank branches still matter? the effect of closings on local economic outcomes. *Department of Economics, Massachusetts Institute of Technology, Cambridge, MA*.

[Nickel et al., 2005] Nickel, S., Puerto, J., and Rodríguez-Chía, A. M. (2005). Mcdm location problems. In *Multiple criteria decision analysis: State of the art surveys*, pages 761–787. Springer.

[Okeahalam, 2009] Okeahalam, C. (2009). Bank branch location: A count analysis. *Spatial economic analysis*, 4(3):275–300.

[Ono et al., 2016] Ono, A., Saito, Y., Sakai, K., Uesugi, I., et al. (2016). Does geographical proximity matter in small business lending? evidence from changes in main bank relationships. Technical report, Institute of Economic Research, Hitotsubashi University.

[Petersen and Rajan, 2002] Petersen, M. A. and Rajan, R. G. (2002). Does distance still matter? the information revolution in small business lending. *The Journal of Finance*, 57(6):2533–2570.

[Ron Martin, 1999] Ron Martin, L. (1999). *Money and the space economy*. Wiley.

[Soenen, 1974] Soenen, L. A. (1974). Locating bank branches. *Industrial Marketing Management*, 3(4):211–227.

[Sokol, 2013] Sokol, M. (2013). Towards a 'newer'economic geography? injecting finance and financialisation into economic geographies. *Cambridge Journal of Regions, Economy and Society*, 6(3):501–515.

[Wilson, 2012] Wilson, A. (2012). *The science of cities and regions: lectures on mathematical model design*. Springer Science & Business Media.

[Zazzaro, 1997] Zazzaro, A. (1997). Regional banking systems, credit allocation and regional economic development. *Economie Appliquée*, 50(1):49–72.

[Zysman, 1984] Zysman, J. (1984). *Governments, markets, and growth: financial systems and the politics of industrial change*, volume 15. Cornell University Press.

Concept index

financial instability, 14

distance, 10–13

economic geography, 6, 8, 17
economic landscape, 13

facality location, 17
financial centers, 6
financial decision, 6
financial economics, 5, 6, 17
financial geography, 5–7, 17
financial instability, 14
financial market, 6

financial markets, 6
financial stability, 8
financial system, 6
functional distance, 11

geographies of money, 14

monetary geography, 14

offshore, 6
onshore, 6
operational distance, 11

spatial distribution, 8

transport cost, 13

Notes

Notes

Notes

Notes

www.ingramcontent.com/pod-product-compliance
Lightning Source LLC
Chambersburg PA
CBHW070912220526
45466CB00005B/2199